I'm a Hero Too®

First published in hardback in 2011

Copyright © Timothy P. Dunnigan 2011

The right of Timothy P. Dunnigan to be identified as the author and Sarah Mills as the

illustrator of this Work has been asserted by them in accordance

with U.S Copyright Law

Printed in the U.S.A

ISBN: 978-0-615-45783-3

CPSIA facility code: BP 311039

I'm a Hero Too

Daddy version

Mommy version also available where this book is sold, or online at **ImaHeroToo.com**

This story is dedicated to all children of military families, past and present - thank you for your many contributions.

The significance of your role in our country's freedom cannot be understated, for it is your support and sacrifice that motivates fathers and mothers in uniform to defend our way of life. It is your heroism this book brings attention to. Our country's path to freedom is not only paved by those who volunteer, but also by those who support them.

Thank *you* for *your* service to our Nation.

Acknowledgements

My inspiration for this book is my children, who have sacrificed numerous times at all different levels, but continue to endure. Thank you for your support and the emotional sacrifices all of you paid in the price of our freedom. Each of you were required to endure prolonged absences as well as face all the challenges of a military lifestyle, yet none of you volunteered. For this reason, it is ultimately your heroism that deserves recognition. From the bottom of my heart, thank you - I love each of you very much.

My wife, Brandy, is the rock upon which I leaned many times during the publishing of this book, as well as throughout my military career. Her advice, support, and contributions are felt across this journey. She too has sacrificed much for my military pursuits. My love, gratitude, and appreciation for her runs very deep. Thank you, Sweetie, I love you.

Shari Mask's insight and writing talents provided me a direction to pursue. In just several sentences, her creative ideas and poignant words gave me a writing foundation upon which I could tell this story. I genuinely appreciate her consult, support, and contributions to this book. Shari is a mother of two adoring daughters, loving wife, gifted writer, and a veteran of our Armed Forces - making her the ideal consult in this developmental family journey. Thank you, Shari.

Sarah Mills' brilliant illustrations are only the surface of her contributions to this book. Her ability to translate my vision, into these beautiful works of art, is amazing. An incredible talent, Sarah is insightful, personable, creative, and professional. I truly appreciate her consult, dedication, and her extraordinary gift. Thank you, Sarah.

Tugger, our French Bulldog, is the most loving, furry comfort a family could ask for. He is featured throughout this story to represent the love a pet brings a military family. Thank you, Tugger - we love you buddy.

Introduction

I'm a Hero Too offers a developmental journey into some of the more common emotions young children face, but find difficult to define or express, in the absence of a military parent. It offers insights to guide the child's desires to be involved with the absent parent through activities and meaningful thoughts. Whether the absence is thirty days for a military school, training rotations, or a one-year unit deployment, our story makes suggestions on how to stay in touch with feelings, emotions, and the absent parent.

The emotional skill-set of a younger child is limited, to say the least. Watching a child not want to eat when you know they're hungry or a tired child not want to sleep, are common amongst children who have a deployed or temporarily absent parent. Many emotions accompany such separations and the longer the absence, the more likely the child's confusion and emotional turmoil. It is the role of the parent or caregiver left behind that faces the daunting task of looking for the signs and symptoms of conflicting feelings that are often hidden and express themselves in emotions such as anger and fear. It is ultimately the responsibility of the caregiver to help the child cope with the absence by encouraging them to identify their feelings and find ways to openly and confidently express them.

I'm a Hero Too was written over an entire military career. It was only when I retired from active duty that I truly viewed the summation of all the sacrifices my children made over the years. Although my younger children are more appreciative of the age-appropriateness of the book, it is no less relevant for my older kids as it was their emotional connection to my career that motivated me to write. You could say this book was inspired by actual events because it tells the story not only of my family's experiences, but also of countless families we interacted with and befriended over a career.

I'm a Hero Too reads and is illustrated purposely as branch immaterial, military nonspecific, and gender neutral - there is a *Daddy* and a *Mommy* version of the book*. All the love, time, and efforts put into writing this very unique book are to ensure that no military child is left out of this story.

*Both versions of this book are available @ Imaherotoo.com

I'm a Hero Too

by
Tim Dunnigan
and **Shari Mask**

illustrations by
Sarah Mills

My daddy keeps our country safe,
and for now he's far away.
I will stay right here at home,
and work hard to be okay.
My daddy is a hero,
with a great big job to do!
He shared with me,
that just like he, I'm a hero too.

I was afraid that he was leaving,
because I did something wrong.
But he shared with me how important I am,
and asked me to be strong.
My daddy is a hero,
and that's a hard thing to be.
Now I know I'm a hero too,
that's a great big job for me!

Sometimes It's hard to be okay,
when my daddy's not at home.
Lucky for me I am very much loved,
and I am not alone.
My family is here with me,
and they miss daddy too.
So together we'll work hard;
we all have a great big job to do!

I miss my daddy while he is gone,
and sometimes feel alone.
But I must remember my daddy needs me,
and soon he will come home.
I have to wait and that takes time.
It's okay to cry and feel sad inside.
It's okay if I don't understand –
I'll still show my love any way that I can.

I know my daddy sometimes worries,
so I'll help him be okay.
I'll work hard to take care of myself,
each and every day.
Sometimes I will be tired,
and I may not want to sleep.
At times I will be hungry,
but may not want to eat.

Sometimes I might get angry,
because my daddy's gone.
I may want to stomp and shout,
and try to do things wrong!
But I'm a hero too,
and I will try not to yell or fight.
Instead I'll work hard each day,
and try to do what's right!

I will remember my daddy loves me,
when I'm sad or feeling down.
I will keep his picture to kiss and hug,
while he is not around.
I miss him so much that sometimes I'm scared,
but I am not alone!
My daddy's with me in my heart,
and soon he will come home!

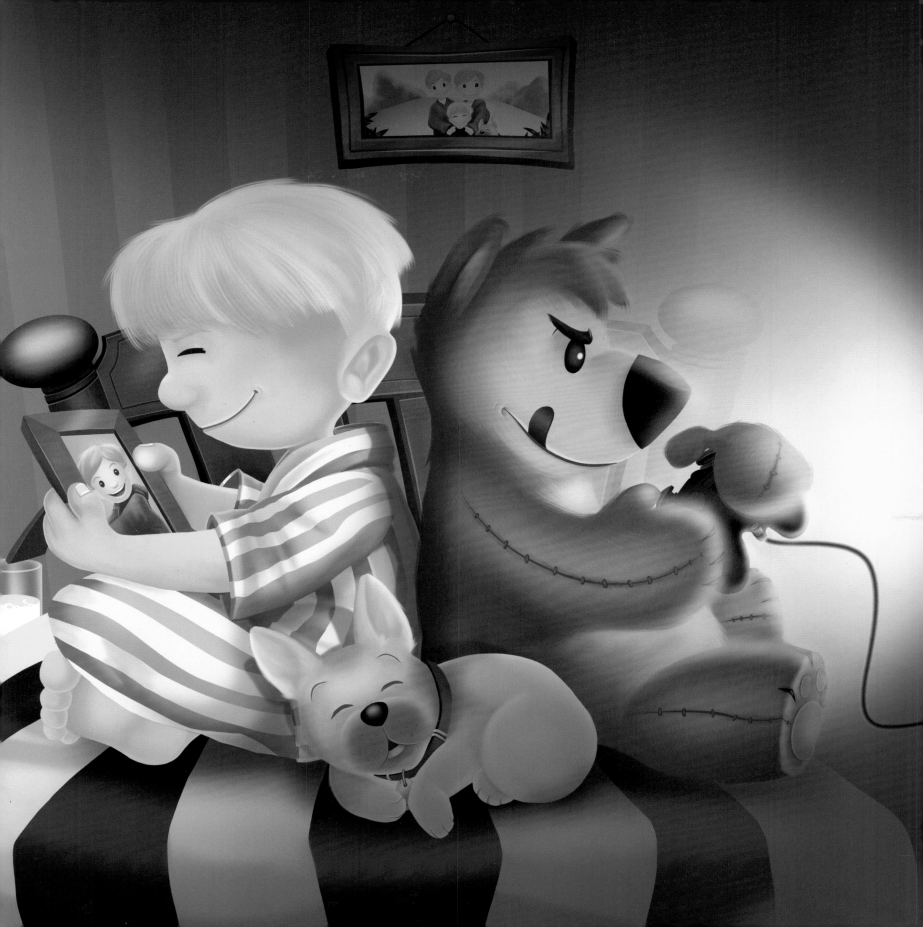

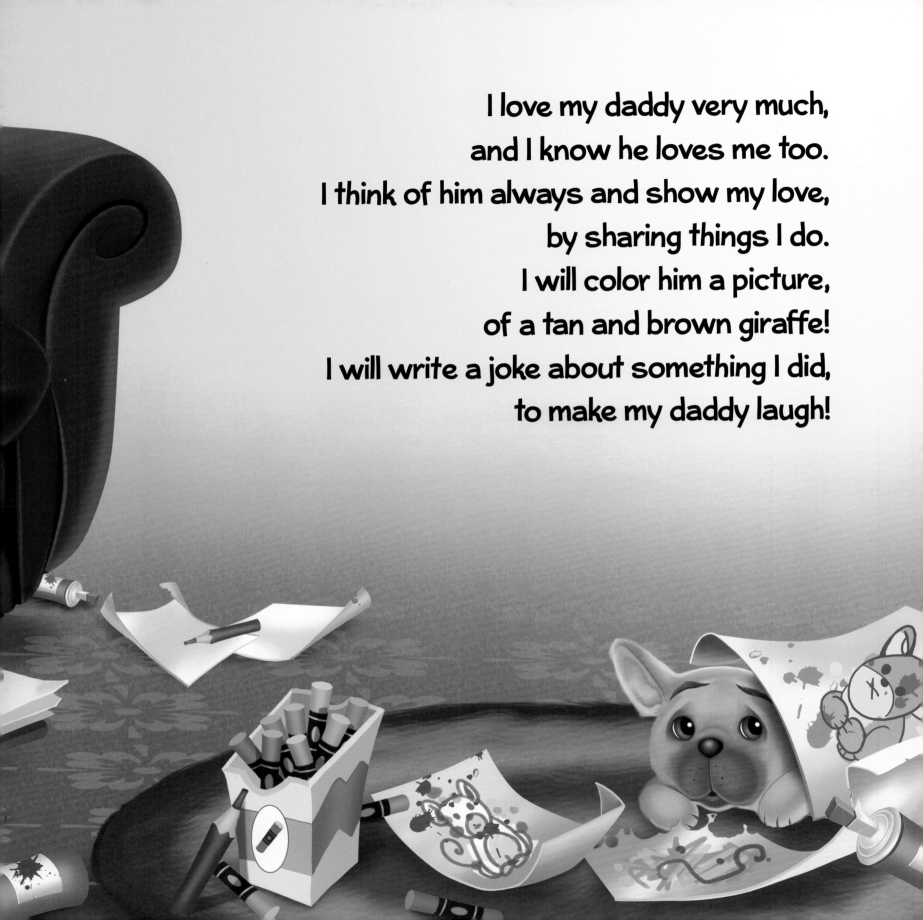

I love my daddy very much,
and I know he loves me too.
I think of him always and show my love,
by sharing things I do.
I will color him a picture,
of a tan and brown giraffe!
I will write a joke about something I did,
to make my daddy laugh!

I'll tell him a story about something I've seen,
and sing him my favorite song!
I'll send him a happy photo of me,
because my smile keeps daddy strong.
I am with my daddy, deep in his heart,
and when I close my eyes he's not so far.
I see his face and feel his hugs,
he does the same to feel my love.

I will close my eyes and imagine a place,
where daddy and me sit face to face.
I will think of the games we like to play,
and remember the things he likes to say.
I will think of him all throughout the day.
I will do these things to be okay!

I am brave and I am strong.
The time will pass – it won't be long.
When daddy comes home he will see,
how hard I've worked and be proud of me.
I will hold our flag and stand real tall,
with a great big smile his name I'll call.
"Daddy! Daddy! Welcome home!"
He'll be surprised at how much I've grown.

I will show him he's my hero,
with a great big hug and kiss!
My daddy will see how happy I am,
no longer will he be missed.
I'm proud of my daddy and my family too;
we all had a great big job to do.
I'm proud of myself for making it through,
and showing my daddy I'm a hero too!

fin